Discovering
ABBEYS AND PRIORIES

Geoffrey N. Wright

Shire Publications Ltd

CONTENTS

Introduction   3

The Earliest Monasteries   5

The Monastic Orders   8

Building Operations   13

The Officers of the Monastery   14

The Lay-out of a Monastery   33

The Daily Life   47

Monasteries and the Landscape   49

The Dissolution   50

Bibliography   52

Monasteries Today   53

Gazetteer of the more important Monastic Remains   54

Index   64

Copyright © 1969 and 1979 by Shire Publications Ltd. First published 1969; reprinted 1970. Second edition 1979; reprinted 1985, 1987. No. 57 in the Discovering series. ISBN 0 85263 454 4.

Printed in Great Britain by C. I. Thomas & Sons (Haverfordwest) Ltd, Merlins Bridge, Haverfordwest.

INTRODUCTION

The word 'abbey' may conjure up different things to different people. To some it may mean the idea of a splendid church, as at Bath, Malmesbury, Selby, Sherborne, Romsey, or Westminster; to others it may bring a vision of an exquisite ruin in very picturesque surroundings, as at Rievaulx, Tintern, or Dryburgh; others may even associate the word with an elegant country mansion as at Lacock, in Wiltshire, and Newstead, in Nottinghamshire. Added to this, many of our famous cathedrals are correctly referred to as 'abbey churches'. Furthermore, some famous ruins are priories—a name also used for some parish churches and, with less justification, for country houses.

All this is rather confusing. The aim of this book is to clarify matters: it explains how our monasteries came into being, with the churches and domestic buildings associated with them, and with the monks whose lives were spent there, up to the Reformation in the first half of the sixteenth century.

Many of our monastic ruins are under the guardianship of the Department of the Environment and are therefore readily accessible to the public. Others may be under private ownership, and accessible at certain times. Many remains of important medieval religious houses are still in ecclesiastical use and can readily be seen. A county-by-county list of the more important monastic remains is given at the end of the book, together with details of what can be seen there. Over two hundred places are listed.

PHOTOGRAPHS
All photographs are by the author, except plates 13 and 17, which are by Jeffery W. Whitelaw, and the cover photograph of Fountains Abbey which is by Cadbury Lamb.

3

*The **abbey** gateway at Bristol
in the eighteenth century.*

THE EARLIEST MONASTERIES

Since the very earliest days of Christianity there have been men who preferred to leave the everyday life of the world in order to devote their lives to prayer and the worship of God. These first monks—the word 'monk' means 'solitary'—lived alone as hermits in lonely caves or in crude cells. When, in time, monks banded together into small communities, monasteries developed.

Christianity first reached Britain during Roman times, and our first Christian martyr was St. Alban, a Roman citizen, after whom the Hertfordshire town of **St. Albans** is named. In the fifth century, when heathen invaders from the continent had overrun our lowlands, the Roman-Celts who had fled westwards to the lonely hills of Cornwall, Wales, and Strathclyde, gained strength from their old Christian faith. They built simple wooden chapels and established tiny monasteries with enclosed grass lawns, or 'llans'—and these places are marked on our maps to-day with the prefixes of 'capel' and 'llan'.

St. Patrick carried this Christian faith to Ireland in the fifth century, and his Irish monks lived in separate tiny cells of earth or stone with thatched roofs, but probably met together for church services and meals. From Ireland, St. Columba carried the faith to Scotland, where he founded a monastery at **Iona,** also a collection of separate cells. From there, the Christian faith spread to the north of England, carried by Columba's monks who, throughout Northumbria, preached, healed, and won the hearts of men. In 597, the year that Columba died, St. Augustine brought Christianity back to the south of England, and established our first Benedictine monastery at **Canterbury,** a very different one from those in the far west and in Northumbria.

The Benedictine Rules

St. Benedict was an Italian monk who had initially lived in a cave as a hermit, but later realised that monks living in a community could serve God more fully than as solitary individuals. In the year 529 he founded the first of his fourteen Italian monasteries, at Monte Cassino, near Naples. In its community his monks lived a life of prayer, hard work, self-discipline, and good deeds, following a set of Rules which Benedict had written out in his own hand. These demanded from the monks vows of poverty, obedience, and chastity,

5

and they also provided a timetable for the monk's day. This was divided into three parts: first, the work of God, carried out by the eight daily services in church; second, the work in the cloisters—meditation, writing, translating, copying manuscripts and illuminating them; third, work in the fields and gardens to provide necessary food and clothing, or in the form of craftsmanship in sculpture, carving, or metalwork.

The Anglo-Saxon Monasteries

St. Augustine's foundation of the great monastery of St. Peter and St. Paul at **Canterbury** started a continuous history of almost a thousand years of Benedictine Rule in Britain. From Canterbury the Roman monks took their missions westwards to Wessex, where **Glastonbury** became the most famous monastery. In the north, Columba's monks had spread their influence, and later disciples of Aidan moved southwards into the Midlands—Mercia, as it was called. By the seventh century England had become a Christian country, and the next century saw the first flowering of our national genius in the earliest churches at **Brixworth** in Northamptonshire, **Escomb** in Durham, and **Bradford-on-Avon** in Wiltshire, as well as in the beautifully-sculptured Celtic crosses at **Bewcastle** in Cumberland, and **Ruthwell,** Dumfries, carved by Northumbrian monks.

These Anglo-Saxon monasteries were famous throughout Europe as centres of learning and the arts. The first English books were copied and decorated by monks in their tiny cells, the most superb of all being the achievements of the Venerable Bede, the greatest eighth century scholar in all Europe. In his little monastery cell at **Jarrow** he wrote a stream of books—on poetry, theology, history, grammar, and science—and the most famous of all his works was his *Ecclesiastical History of the English Nation*—clear, just and learned. Bede introduced to England the idea of dating years from the birth of Christ, and he left to his countrymen the earliest translation of the Gospel of St. John into their own language—the last sentences of which he dictated as he lay dying on the floor of his monastery cell. Bede is now buried in **Durham Cathedral,** the great monastic building dedicated to another north country monk, St. Cuthbert, who had become Bishop of Lindisfarne, where the exquisitely lovely Lindisfarne Gospel had been produced. This remarkable work is now in the British Museum. The monastic church in which Bede worshipped survives as the sanctuary of St Paul's church, **Jarrow.**

Two centuries of Danish invasions, from the eighth to the tenth centuries, brought regular monastic life to an end, and it was not until the second half of the tenth century that its revival became possible. The monasteries of Northumbria and the Fen country had by then been destroyed, and only those at **Canterbury** and in the Celtic west had survived.

A Wessex monk, Dunstan, became Abbot of **Glastonbury,** where he soon made his monastery famous throughout England for its music, its teaching, and its services. In 960 he was made Archbishop of Canterbury, and, with his great reformers Ethelwold, Bishop of **Winchester,** and Oswald, Bishop of **York,** he was largely responsible for reviving Benedictine Rule in its original form, at **Bath, Worcester, Cerne, Abingdon, Winchcombe, Eynsham, Crowland, Peterborough, Ely, Bury St. Edmunds,** as well as **Winchester** and **Glastonbury** itself. By the time of the Norman Conquest there were thirty-five monasteries and nine nunneries, all Benedictine.

A Benedictine monk

THE MONASTIC ORDERS

Until about A.D. 1100 the only monasteries in the western Church, apart from the few surviving Celtic ones, followed the Benedictine Rule. But towards the end of the eleventh century, and in the following one, monasticism grew very rapidly, hundreds of new monasteries were built, and several new monastic Orders were founded. Most of these arose from the fact that many existing Benedictine monasteries had become both worldly and wealthy, and the new Orders represented a return to the simpler and stricter rules of monastic life which St. Benedict had originally laid down.

Thus, the new Orders, differing only in their interpretations of the Rule, were called after the monastic houses which had made the various breakaways. Most of these were in France, and from those at Citeaux and Cluny we have got the anglicised Cistercian and Cluniac Orders.

The Cistercians

Citeaux Abbey had been founded at the end of the eleventh century, and its set of rules was drawn up by an English abbot, Stephen Harding, of Dorset, with Bernard, a young French nobleman. The Cistercian Order was a strict one, and its Rule would not allow its monks to build monasteries in towns. Instead, wild places far away from worldly affairs had to be chosen. The first Cistercian foundation in England was at **Waverley,** two miles south-east of Farnham in Surrey, established in 1128, and of which practically nothing above ground remains. The main expansion of the Cistercian Order took place in the north of England and in Wales, where few Benedictine monasteries existed, and where vast areas of wild and uncultivated land gave the Cistercian monks the necessary opportunities for their pioneering endeavours.

Unlike the Benedictines, the Cistercians insisted on hard manual work, and accepted no gifts other than land. Thus they became great farmers, and on the northern and Welsh hills they kept thousands of sheep, whose wool was subsequently sold to pay for the erection of their monastic churches. Their Rule initially forbade them use of any ornament or decoration in their churches, but this was later relaxed. They were allowed only to wear robes of coarse white cloth, and the wearing of this habit resulted in their being called the White Monks, as opposed to the Black Monks, which was the name given to the Benedictines and later to the Cluniacs.

Cistercian monks lived lives of hard work, silence, and prayer, and, being of necessity self-supporting, they developed great skills, not only in farming and shepherding, but also in the construction of mills and water-courses for the use of the monastery. They mined metal ores from the Yorkshire hills, they established local industries, and they even owned boats with which overseas trade was carried out.

The Cistercian Order did not allow the employment of servants, but, as it did attract quite large numbers of uneducated men from rural districts, the monks were divided into two classes—the choir-monks, who attended all church services and looked after the running of the monastery, and the lay-brothers, who did most of the heavy labour and the farm-work. Because the Cistercians acquired vast estates, particularly on the Pennines and the Yorkshire Moors, some of the farmlands were too distant to be worked from the monastery, so outlying cells, with barns and stables, were built—called granges—and these were looked after by the lay-brothers. For example, much of Borrowdale, in the Lake District, belonged to **Furness Abbey,** some 30 miles away, and the village of Grange-in-Borrowdale got its name from the fact that a monastic grange of the abbey had been established there by the thirteenth century.

Between 1128 and 1152, when the first period of Cistercian settlement had come to an end, about fifty Cistercian monasteries had been founded. Of each of them it could reasonably be said that the monks had taken over a wilderness and turned it into a garden or, more accurately, into a sheep-run. This was certainly the case over much of northern England, where the wool production on the Cistercian estates led to a medieval export trade which made such a big contribution to our national prosperity throughout the Middle Ages. The Cistercians shared in this prosperity, so that they, too, became rich without wanting to, and much of their original zeal and strictness gradually vanished. Beautiful towers were added to their churches, exemplified at **Fountains Abbey** by Abbot Huby's tower of about 1500.

Large Cistercian foundations such as **Fountains** or **Rievaulx** might have accommodated as many as 150 choir-monks and 500 lay-brothers at the height of their prosperity in the thirteenth century. Of the seventy-five Cistercian abbeys, and twenty-six nunneries, which were eventually established, few were as enormous as this, but nevertheless these numbers do give some indication of the vastness and importance to the community of Cistercian foundations in remote places.

The Cluniacs

Although the Cluniac Order had been founded as long ago as 910, at Cluny, in France, its influence did not spread until the Norman Conquest. Monks of this Order wore a black habit, like the Benedictines, and devoted much of their time to church services, and left work in the gardens and fields to paid servants. **Lewes** in Sussex was the first Cluniac foundation in this country, and by 1160 there were thirty-six Cluniac houses, mostly very small cells housing only four or five monks. **Castle Acre** and **Thetford** (Norfolk) and **Much Wenlock** (Shropshire) are good surviving larger Cluniac foundations.

The Carthusians

The Carthusian Order takes its name from the French town of Chartreuse, where the first Carthusian monastery was founded by St. Bruno in the twelfth century. It represented a breakaway from the Cluniacs, and aimed at a yet more simple and severe life of purity and piety. Carthusian monks lived in almost complete solitude and complete silence, rather in the manner of the early hermits, yet still belonging to a community. Each monk had his little cottage-like cell with study and bedroom, and a walled garden behind, with the front door of his cell opening out on to a broad cloister. At the side of the door was a hatch where his food would be left, twice a day, by a lay-brother whom he never saw and never spoke to. A Carthusian monk was allowed to possess only a few things—pen, ink, books, razor, needle and thread, a white robe and a coarse shirt to irritate his flesh so that he might learn to accept hardship and privation cheerfully.

The day would be spent in prayer and meditation, and working in the garden, and the austerity of the Carthusian Order was such that it was never in need of reform or improvement. The monks would meet in church for service each day, but would not speak to one another. It was only on rare occasions that conversation was permitted, perhaps during an occasional communal meal, and then under the observation of the prior.

Because of the severity of the Rule, the Carthusian Order never became popular, and there were only nine Carthusian houses in England. The first of these was at Witham, in Somerset, of which practically nothing remains. Only at **Mount Grace,** in the North Riding, founded in 1398, is there a good lay-out of a Carthusian priory, and it really is an excellent one, including a rebuilt monk's cell in the cloister. **Hinton,** south of Bath, retains its chapter-house, while the

London Charter House became the Charterhouse School.

Black Canons and White Canons

The monasteries mentioned up to now followed the Rule of St. Benedict, with varied interpretations from one Order to another. They were houses of monks whose lives were spent within the monastic communities. Two other types of monasteries existed, peopled by Canons Regular. These canons lived in communities, like the monks, but, unlike them, went out preaching. Indeed, their monasteries served as centres of parochial activity, and their monks were priests who observed the Rule of St. Augustine, Bishop of Hippo. They first appeared in England about 1100, where a community of Augustinians established itself at **Colchester,** where they built their monastery largely of available bricks from the old Roman town. Much of their church still stands, as **St. Botolph's Priory.** The Augustinians were also known as the Austin Canons, and, wearing a black habit like the Benedictine monks, became called the Black Canons. Many of their splendid churches survive, and are still in use, their large naves being evidence of the big congregations the Augustinians attracted—as at **Bristol** and **Carlisle** cathedrals, and the priories of **Bolton, Lanercost, Christchurch** (Dorset), **Cartmel** and **Dorchester Abbey.** Generally speaking, the Augustinians lived in comparative comfort, and certainly on a much more liberal scale than the monks, being especially generous in their hospitality.

A second Order, following more austere ways of life, was formed at Premontre, in France, in 1123, and, being more akin to the Cistercians than the Benedictines, chose to wear a white habit. These Premonstratensians—more easily thought of as the White Canons—established their first English house at **Alnwick** in 1147, and eventually founded thirty-one abbeys and two nunneries throughout the country, only a few surviving as ruins to-day, **Easby** (N. Yorks), **Egglestone** (Durham), **Shap** (Cumbria), **Titchfield** (Hants) and **Bayham** (Sussex) being the best.

Nuns

During the Middle Ages there were over a hundred nunneries in England, but for the most part they were neither as wealthy nor as important as the bigger monasteries. They were usually small houses, and rather poor, mainly because the nuns could not undertake the type of farmwork which made the Cistercians wealthy, but also because they did not attract large gifts of money or land, except in the cases of **Romsey** in Hampshire, and **Barking** in London.

A Cistercian monk

Romsey Abbey, like most of the houses of nuns, was a Benedictine foundation, and its church is the finest of all the nun's churches. The best remaining monastic buildings of a nunnery are those at **Lacock Abbey** in Wiltshire, which was a house of Augustinian canonesses, founded by the Countess Ela of Salisbury on the same day in 1232 as she also founded the Carthusian house at **Hinton,** a dozen miles to the west, south of Bath.

Most nunneries were priories, in charge of a prioress, and under the overall rule of a monastery of the same Order. Their inmates were very often women from quite well-to-do homes who had failed to find a husband. After some years as spinsters, and helping to bring up younger brothers and sisters, they were expected to 'take the veil' without really wanting to do so. In the nunnery, apart from the church services which they had to attend, nuns would spend much of their time weaving or spinning wool and linen for their own clothes, and embroidering the church vestments. Rarely having been so educated as men, they were not expected to spend a lot of time in the cloisters reading and writing.

Double Houses

Gilbert of Sempringham, a twelfth century Lincolnshire priest, was the only Englishman to found his own Order. He established a convent for seven unmarried women of his parish, under Benedictine Rule, spiritually ministered to by a small house of Augustinian canons. Lay brothers and lay sisters did manual work. Eventually, twenty-six Gilbertine double-houses had been founded, half of them during Gilbert's own lifetime. In them, canons and nuns had separate cloisters, but worshipped together in one church, albeit with a wall high enough to prevent their seeing each other. These Gilbertine houses were ruled jointly by a prior and a prioress. Another similar Order, the Bridgettines, had only one English house, **Syon Abbey** in Middlesex.

BUILDING OPERATIONS

In medieval times the monastic ideal of life was regarded as of the highest importance. As a result, there was rarely a shortage of funds to pay for the building of the monasteries, or for their endowment. Income came chiefly from the possessions of the chapter, in land, property, and benefices. Offerings made at the altar and at saints' shrines often amounted to a considerable sum, while miracle-working relics and roods, such as St. Edmund's bones at **Bury St. Edmunds** and the roods at **Malmesbury** and **Bermondsey,** brought numerous gifts.

The early monasteries were erected very largely by the monks themselves but it was not long before their design and building passed into the more capable hands of professional lay craftsmen. As with any major building, an architect, called the master-mason, was appointed to take overall control. Decisions about position, size, and style of building would initially need the approval of the abbot or prior, who, with the sacrist, would also handle the financial aspect. But the work itself, the employment of itinerant masons and other craftsmen, was the responsibility of the master-mason. Rough masons worked the big stone blocks, and reduced them to a manageable size; higher-paid and very much more skilled freemasons handled the freestone, working with mallet and chisel, moulded the arches, cut the delicate tracery, and did much of the carving. Individual gifted monks also undertook the skilled work of carving, but most of the work was in lay hands. As an example of cost, the eastern half of Westminster Abbey built between 1245 and 1269, cost **King Henry III £50,000.**

THE OFFICERS OF THE MONASTERY

The community of monks—or nuns—living together is called a religious house, or convent. A religious house of monks is a monastery, and of nuns a nunnery. Both monasteries and nunneries could be called abbeys or priories, the distinction being purely one of status. An abbey of monks would have as its head an abbot, or if of nuns, an abbess. A priory would have no resident abbot but would be presided over by a prior or prioress, and in most cases was an offshoot from, and dependent upon, an abbey. Houses of regular canons living under monastic rule were also classified as abbeys and priories.

The **Abbot** was the head of the monastery and was chosen by the monks themselves, for his goodness, his wisdom, and his leadership. He had to be a father to the monks, his word was law, and he had to be well educated in order to deal with all the wide range of monastic affairs and responsibilities. When, at first, the monasteries were small, the abbot lived, worked, and even slept with his brother-monks. But as a monastery grew in size and importance he became a greater man, perhaps lord of one or more manors, a big landowner, and a friend of noblemen and even kings. By then it became necessary for him to have his own house, the abbot's lodging, within the precinct, where he could entertain important guests and other monastic heads, although he did, from time to time, invite monks in his own house to join him at table.

Next in importance to the abbot was the **Prior.** In a big monastery he would frequently have to take charge of the affairs during the absences of the abbot; in the case of a priory he would be in complete charge, having been seconded to it from the mother-abbey. The prior had an assistant called the **Sub-Prior,** and under him were the monks of the house who had special duties. These monks were called **Obedientiaries.**

Each obedientiary had a specific job for which he was responsible. The church being the most important monastic building, the monk in charge of its services would be the most important obedientiary. He was called the **Precentor,** made arrangements for all the services, was in charge of the music and the choir-books, trained the monks to sing, decided the readings for the services, and even had to provide materials for writing and repairing books from the choir and the cloister.

The **Sacristan** looked after the contents of the church, the vestments worn, the valuable linen, the embroidered robes and banners, the gold and silver plate, and the holy vessels of the altar. His chief helper, the **Sub-Sacristan,** had the extra responsibility of ringing the bell for each of the services throughout the day. Some monasteries possessed very valuable plate and holy relics, usually kept in a special container called the reliquary. Pilgrims sometimes travelled long distances to see these relics. At **St. Albans** this reliquary and the nearby watching-loft for the sacristan can still be seen.

The claustral life of the monastery was in the hands of a number of obedientiaries. The **Cellarer** looked after the cellars and stores, housed in the undercroft, usually beneath the west range of the cloister. All the monastic supplies of food, ale, and wines were stored there, in the cellarium. The best example of this building is the huge vaulted structure at **Fountains Abbey.** The cellarer would have to meet tradesmen, probably in the slype which led from either the east or west sides of the cloister, in order to buy or sell produce. He also looked after the bakehouse and the brewhouse, assisted by the **Sub-Cellarer.**

The **Kitchener** was in charge of the kitchens where the food was cooked, and the **Fraterer,** or **Refectorian,** looked after the serving of food in the frater, as well as seeing that clean towels were provided at the lavatorium, fresh rushes for the frater floor, and lamps during the dark days and evenings of winter. Servants waited on the monks in the frater.

The other buildings around the cloister were the responsibility of the **Chamberlain,** whose job it was to see that the bedding in the monks' dorter was adequate and in good condition. He also had to provide the monks' habits, their boots and shoes, and their linen. He also arranged the hot-water supply for the washing of feet, usually on Saturdays, for the shaving of heads every three weeks, and baths perhaps once a quarter. In winter he had to see that the fire in the calefactory was kept well-stoked up.

Monks who were old or sick lived in the infirmary, a separate building away from the cloister, but still within the precinct of the monastery. The **Infirmarian** was in charge of this building, with its long room like a present-day hospital ward, and beds down each side. Sick monks were allowed to eat flesh-meat, something normally denied their more healthy brothers, and the infirmary's own dining-room was entirely separate from the main frater, and was called the misericord.

Because they were constantly tending the sick the infirmarian and his assistants gained considerable medical skill, a good knowledge of first-aid, and the ability to perform simple operations. As a result, lay-people from outside the monastery came to the monasteries for treatment of illnesses, and payments for this would go towards providing better buildings. Medicines and ointments were made from herbs grown specially in the monastery herb-garden.

In the Middle Ages many people were very poor, and one of the main tasks of a monastery was to help them. The **Almoner** was responsible for this care of the poor, and he gave away scraps of food from the kitchen, worn clothing and other materials, to the folk who queued up each day for their 'dole'. Some monasteries fed an exact number of people each day, giving them, perhaps, 'a mess of pottage (peas and beans), a farthing loaf, and a farthingsworth of beer.'

The **Hospitaller,** or **Guest-Master,** dispensed hospitality to the many visitors and pilgrims who came to the monastery. Such travellers would be given a bed and a meal in the guest-house, or, if they were poor, in the almonry. In either case, they were not expected to pay unless they wanted to, since the monastery regarded the hospitality to wayfarers as part of their duty. Important guests would, of course, be entertained in the abbot's lodging. Care of travellers even extended in some cases to the provision and upkeep of roads leading to the monastery.

The **Master of the Novices** was the monk in charge of the boys and young men who were learning to become monks. First, a **Novice** would have the top of his head shaved bare—the 'tonsure'—then he received his habit, a long robe with wide sleeves and a hood (black for Benedictines, white for Cistercians). Preparation for monk-hood and lessons in the cloisters would last at least a year for the young men, and more for boys, and after it the novice would make his vows, of poverty, obedience, and chastity. Then he would get his monk's cowl (a very big hood) and would be one of the monks of the convent or religious house.

1. Lindisfarne Priory on Holy Island, off the Northumberland coast.

2. Fountains Abbey, North Yorkshire: the church and cloister range from the west (twelfth and thirteenth centuries). The tower was added in the early sixteenth century.
3. Mount Grace Priory, North Yorkshire: a reconstructed monk's cell.

4. Downside Abbey, Somerset, and some of the buildings of Downside School.

5. Tisbury, Wiltshire: the fifteenth-century tithe barn built for the Abbess of Shaftesbury.

6. Glastonbury Abbey, Somerset: the Abbot's Kitchen is one of the best preserved medieval kitchens in Europe.

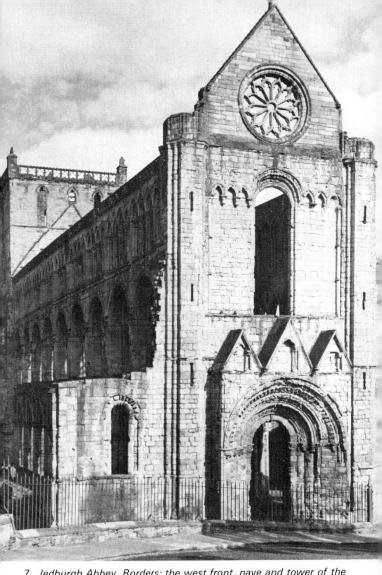

7. *Jedburgh Abbey, Borders: the west front, nave and tower of the late twelfth-century church.*

8. Llanthony Priory, Gwent: an Augustinian house founded in the twelfth century in a remote valley in the Black Mountains.

9. Muchelney Abbey, Somerset: the abbot's lodging and inner wall of the refectory.

10. Malmesbury Abbey, Wiltshire, is now the town's parish church.

11. Tewkesbury Abbey, Gloucestershire, was bought by the townsfolk for £453 after the Dissolution for use as their parish church.

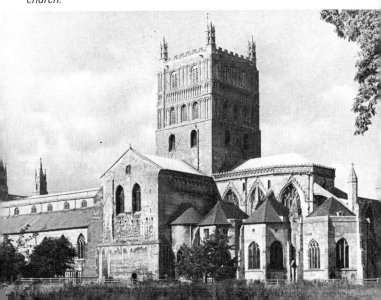

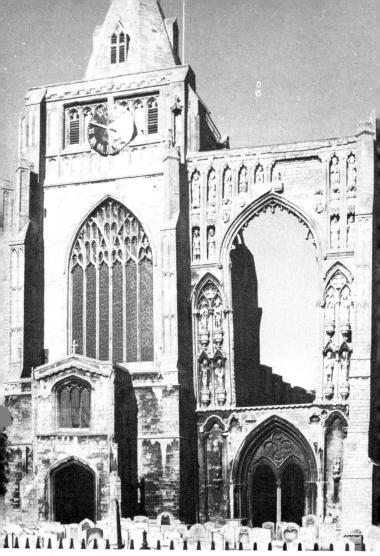

12. *Crowland Abbey, Lincolnshire: the late thirteenth-century west front showing the north aisle, now used as the parish church.*

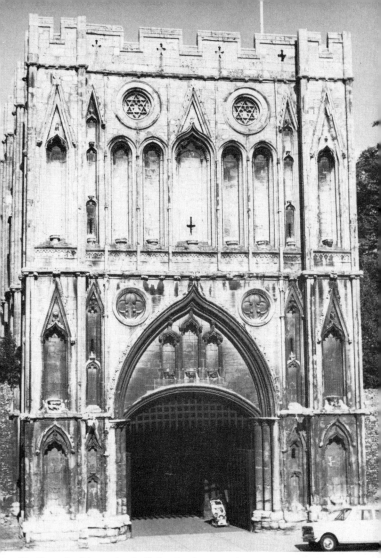

13. Bury St Edmunds, Suffolk: the fourteenth-century gateway to the abbey.

14. *Tintern Abbey, Gwent, in the Wye Valley, was founded by Cistercians in 1131.*

15. *Furness Abbey, Cumbria: cloister arches of c. 1230-40.*

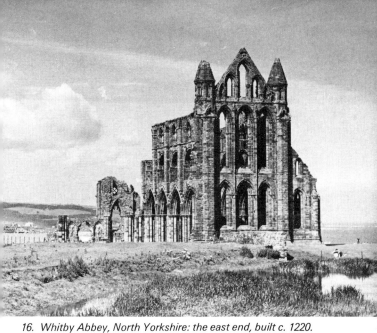

16. *Whitby Abbey, North Yorkshire: the east end, built c. 1220.*

17. *Westminster Abbey, London: the west towers were added by Hawksmoor in 1735-40.*

18. Woodspring Priory, Avon: the church has been made into a private house.

19. Cleeve Abbey, Somerset: the cloister range showing the monks' dorter and night stair.

20. Cleeve Abbey, Somerset: the early sixteenth-century refectory or frater.

21. *Lacock Abbey, Wiltshire: Tudor additions to the cloister after the Dissolution.*

22. *Melrose Abbey, Borders: fine ruins of a twelfth-century abbey.*

23. Sherborne, Dorset: the town conduit in the Market Place was formerly the lavatorium in the abbey cloister (sixteenth century).

24. Fountains Abbey, North Yorkshire: the cellarium.

25. Rievaulx Abbey, North Yorkshire: the chancel was built c. 1225-40.

THE LAY-OUT OF A MONASTERY

By 1066 the lay-out of all monasteries of monks and canons had become standardized. Within the basic plan there were some small, but regular differences between the houses of the Black Monks and those of the White Monks, while the Carthusians were exceptionally different. In addition, differences of siting between the various monasteries brought about local variations in the basic plan. Monastic plans in this country followed the Continental pattern and not the old English one. Any Saxon monasteries remaining at the Norman Conquest were pulled down and replaced by bigger and grander structures.

The essential parts of the monastic plan were the great church, the claustral buildings around which the monks lived, the buildings where they looked after their sick, and showed hospitality to guests, and the curia, or great court, in whose buildings were carried out the day-to-day administration of the monastery, and its estates, and where it also made contact with the outside world.

The medieval arrangement of these four main parts of a monastery showed a Norman genius for planning in that it was both practical and quite simple. The church stood on the highest ground, its nave forming one side of a quadrangle called the cloister. Round the other three sides of this cloister were the buildings (the 'claustral' buildings) where the monks lived, ate, and slept. The administrative buildings, and those where outside contact was made, were grouped in the outer courtyard—the 'curia'—west of the cloister ; the infirmary lay to the east, in the quietest and most peaceful part of the site. The complete lay-out was usually enclosed by a precinct wall, entry through which was by one or more gatehouses. Whenever a monastery was built, the church was built first, starting at the east end with the high altar and the monks' quire, together with the eastern range of the cloister, including the chapter-house and monks' dormitory.

The Church

As this was the building round which the monastery grew, and the place in which more than half the waking hours of the monks were spent in the service of God, it was the most important building of the monastery. In all but the very smallest monasteries the church was planned in the form of a cross—a 'cruciform' shape. This consisted of, from east to west, a Presbytery, a choir, transepts (often with chapels on

33

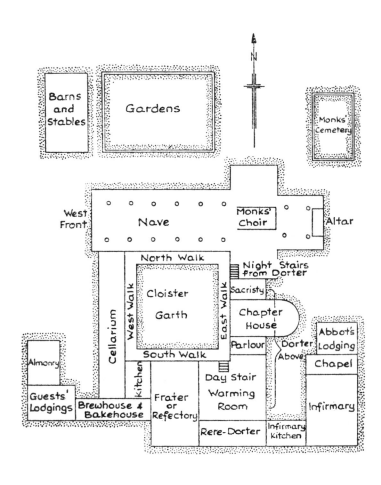

SKETCH PLAN OF MEDIEVAL MONASTERY

their eastern sides), and a nave. The presbytery housed the high altar and was for important ceremonies connected with it. The transepts were mainly for movement and communication. The nave was for the use of servants, lay brothers (in Cistercian monasteries), and in many cases, for the local laity of the adjoining parish.

Norman presbyteries were not very long, extending to two, three or four bays, and ending in an apse. They would usually have an aisle on each side, this aisle being continued round the back of the apse to form a processional path, as at **Gloucester, Norwich, Tewkesbury,** and St. Bartholomew's, at **Smithfield,** in London. As church ceremonial developed to include magnificent choral masses and services specially in honour of the Virgin Mary, special chapels were built for this purpose—called Lady Chapels. Usually these were added on to the east end of the presbytery, as at **Gloucester, Winchester** and **Christchurch,** but special conditions demanded their building on to the west end as at **Durham** and **Glastonbury.**

These more elaborate presbyteries were only suitable for the larger abbey churches. Smaller buildings had square-ended presbyteries with either very short aisles, or no aisles at all. The Benedictines had no aisle in the priory at **Lindisfarne,** nor had the Augustinians at **Bolton Priory,** and the Premonstratensians at **Easby Abbey.**

The churches of all Cistercian monasteries were dedicated to the Virgin Mary, so did not need any Lady chapels. The earlier ones were structurally as simple as a cruciform plan could be, with short, aisleless presbytery, short transepts with rectangular chapels on the east, and an aisleless nave. These very short presbyteries of early Cistercian simplicity are represented at **Kirkstall** and **Valle Crucis.**

However, as Cistercian austerity gradually relaxed during the twelfth century, the shape of the presbytery developed and grew. At **Abbey Dore,** there was an aisled presbytery of three bays, with a row of five chapels beyond it. The extended presbytery became the pride of the great northern abbeys of all Orders—Augustinian **Thornton** had six bays, Benedictine **Whitby** and Cistercian **Rievaulx** had seven bays, Augustinian **Carlisle** and **Kirkham** had eight bays, while Benedictine **York** went to nine. Cistercian **Fountains** added to its aisled presbytery of five bays a spectacular eastern transept, later copied by **Durham,** and famous at both places as the Chapel of the Nine Altars.

The choir lay to the west of the presbytery, usually filling the space of the crossing and the first eastern bays of the nave—still apparent at **Gloucester** and **Westminster.** This monks' choir was separated from the nave by a double screen with a central doorway, and altars on each side of this on the western face. The screen was called the pulpitum, and from it the epistle and gospel would be read at certain times; the organ was often situated above it. **Norwich** has a restored pulpitum of stone, while **Hexham** has a splendid wooden one.

The monks' stalls faced each other along both sides of the choir, and on each side of the pulpitum doorway, with the abbot sitting on the south side of the doorway and the prior on the north.

The transept nearest to the cloister (usually the south one) usually contained the night stairs leading to the adjoining monks' dormitory (dorter), thus making for easy access for the monks to the church for services in the night hours. Few complete examples of night stairs have survived, and by far the best is at **Hexham.** Traces of the night stairs can be identified at various monastic ruins, for example at **Rievaulx.** Cluniac monasteries such as **Castle Acre, Thetford** and **Much Wenlock** dispensed with night stairs completely, so that there was no direct communication between the monks' dormitory and the church.

The nave of the church was always built last. Sometimes it took so long that the style of the building changed, from Norman to early Gothic, before the job was finished, as at **Peterborough, Romsey** and **Selby.** In the greater abbey churches of both Benedictine and Cistercian foundation the nave was often very long—seven bays as at **Buildwas** and **Blyth,** eight at **Durham** and **Roche,** nine at **Binham** and **Rievaulx,** ten at **St. Albans** and **Furness,** eleven at **Fountains** and **Peterborough,** twelve bays at **Byland** and **Winchester,** and at **Norwich** it reached to fourteen bays. Cistercian naves were long in order to house the lay-brothers. In Benedictine churches and those of the Augustinian canons the nave was open for lay people, and in some cases where the rest of the church was destroyed at the Dissolution this parochial use of the nave, or even of an aisle, helped to keep it in use. This has occurred at **Binham, Bridlington, Dunstable, Elstow, Nun Monkton,** and **Tynemouth,** to name a few, while at **Romsey, Leominster, Tewkesbury, Blyth** and **Cartmel** a separate aisle was provided for the lay-folk of the parish.

For special processions on church festivals the west door of the nave would be used. Only a few monasteries were without this entrance—these included **Cartmel, Buildwas, Furness** and **Romsey.** Most of them possessed in addition to this western portal another doorway to the nave, for lay use, near the west end of the church on the opposite side to the cloister. This doorway often had a porch to protect it, the most splendid example being that at **Malmesbury,** showing superb Norman carving. Later examples can be seen at **Canterbury, Chester, Great Malvern** and **Gloucester.**

Most monastic churches were graced by the addition of towers, either a single one over the crossing, or two—one at the crossing and one at the west end of the nave, or even three, with two at the west. Early central towers were always low ones, as at **Winchester, Buildwas** and **Romsey.** Subsequent ones were surmounted by rather squat pyramidal roofs, and in later years the towers were built higher—not always on the best foundations, as a result of which many collapsed—at **Bourne, Bridlington** and **Worksop,** where, in each case, the west tower survived. **Evesham** built a separate tower to house the bells in the early sixteenth century, and this detached structure still stands. Early Cistercian churches were forbidden towers as being too decorative and elaborate, and not in keeping with Cistercian ideals, but as these ideals became relaxed towers came into being. Most stately of them is that built by Abbot Huby at **Fountains** about 1500, erected at the end of the north transept because the central tower was beginning to collapse.

Many monasteries possessed shrines housing the relics of saints. Best-known are those of St. Thomas à Becket at **Canterbury,** St. Cuthbert at **Durham** and St. Edward the Confessor at **Westminster.** The shrines were normally given a position of honour, behind the high altar and near the entrance to the Lady chapel.

Friars' Churches

By the beginning of the thirteenth century, when Cistercian austerity was waning, there was little difference in either plan or elevation between the abbey churches of Benedictine and Cistercian Orders. But the friars, whose main duty of preaching distinguished them from the monks and canons, built large churches specially for that purpose, having wide aisles and broad arcades to the naves, with choirs which were without aisles, although very long.

The Cloisters

Although architecturally speaking the church was the grandest building in the monastery, and was its spiritual centre, representing indeed the main reason for its existence as a monastery, the cloister and its associated buildings deserve the fullest study, so that the monks can be seen, as it were, in the framework of their own society. The monks' vows of poverty, obedience and chastity shut them off from the world, and confined them within the cloister garth or lawn and its immediate surroundings.

The position of the cloister in relation to the church depended on the lie of the land, and the direction of the nearest flowing water for drainage. Ideally, the site for a Cistercian or Premonstratensian monastery would be one on rising ground to the north of a river or stream flowing from west to east. These conditions were obtained naturally at **Fountains,** and artificially at **Dryburgh.** Where conditions did allow, the cloister was placed on the south side of the nave of the church, to catch the sun, and to avoid being in shadow of the roofs of high buildings. The awkward position of the river at **Tintern** and **Buildwas** caused the cloister to be built to the north of the church. Many Benedictine abbeys were situated in towns, very rarely being on virgin sites. Hence they showed planning idiosyncrasies, too, and north-side cloisters exist at **Canterbury, Chester, Gloucester** and **Bury St. Edmunds.** At **Rochester** it is even against the eastern arm of the nave.

Each of the four sides of the cloister had a covered alley of one storey, having a lean-to type of roof to the adjoining wall of church or other building. Early cloisters had open arcades along the side facing the garth, standing on low walls. Small reconstructed portions of these arcades can be seen at **Rievaulx** and **Newminster.** Cloisters built after the introduction of tracery had their open arcades replaced by windows, the later ones being glazed.

Cloisters served many purposes. Primarily they were galleries of communication between the various domestic buildings themselves, and between them and the church. The cloister alley next to the church wall was the recognised place for meditation, and the monks would spend their allotted periods of prayer, reading, study, and meditation in that alley. Some cloisters had stone benches along the church wall for the monks to sit on. The outer wall of this alley was divided into carrels, each carrel occupying the space of half a window. Carrels themselves were separated by wainscoting, and contained a desk for books. **Gloucester** and **Chester** both show these carrels.

A rare Cistercian survival associated with these study periods, particularly with the reading before evening Compline, called the Collation, is the abbot's seat against the church wall half-way along the cloister alley nearest to the church. **Cleeve** possesses the best example of the arched recess for the abbot's chair, while **Tintern** has an easily-identifiable one.

The range of buildings adjoining the eastern alleyway of the cloister was usually of two storeys, all of the upper floor forming the dorter, or monks' dormitory, with a doorway leading to the night stairs in the nearby transept. Few of these dorters still retain their floors and roofs, and those which do use them for other purposes, such as **Durham** and **Westminster** which house libraries, and those at **Cleeve** and **Valle Crucis** which were turned into domestic use by later inhabitants.

The rere-dorter, or necessarium, or latrine-block of the monastery was placed at the end of the dorter furthest from the church, usually jutting out at right-angles from the dorter, or extending across its end as at **Lewes** and **Castle Acre.** Obviously, its position was governed by the course of the main drain, which was channelled along a walled-in course, often constructed with fine masonry as it was of manifest importance. Above this drain, carrying running-water, the rere-dorter was a long, narrow building with a row of stone seats against the wall, each with a window, and divided from the next by a partition. Where the dorter was in an unusual position, as at **Easby** and **Worcester,** where it was in the western range of buildings, this was due entirely to the need for placing it most convenient to the main drain. This influence of drainage on the monastic lay-out is best seen at **Kirkham,** where the drain follows a quarter-circle south-east of the cloister, and a long crescent of buildings—rere-dorter, kitchens, prior's lodging and infirmary follow its course.

The chapter-house was the most important of the eastern range of buildings, regarded as second in importance to the church. The dormitory ran either above it, or above its entrance lobby. Early chapter-houses were regarded as sufficiently sacred for the burial of abbots. The twelfth century chapter-house at **Rievaulx** is unique in containing the shrine of the first abbot, William, erected a century after his death. No other English chapter-house contains such a treasure.

The name 'chapter-house' comes from the fact that, after each daily Morrow Mass at 8 a.m. the monks assembled there for a sort of business meeting, which began with a reading, and always included a chapter from St. Benedict's Rules. This would be followed by lists of the daily and weekly duties of monks. Obituaries of the day, confessions of faults would be heard, and resultant punishments decreed. In addition, the temporal business of the monastery would be carried out in the chapter-house.

Because they were so important, chapter-houses were often constructed with great architectural dignity and elegance, this elaboration being shown at **Bristol** and **Much Wenlock** by rows of beautiful internal arcading. There are other good examples at **Hinton Charterhouse, Chester, Haughmond, Furness,** with polygonal ones at **Westminster, Worcester** and **Cockersand.**

The ground-floor of the dorter range was usually divided into a number of rooms, each leading on to the cloister. The slype came nearest to the transept. This was a passage leading through the range to the east of the church where the monks' cemetery was sited. This passage sometimes served the purpose of a parlour, where limited conversation could take place. Elsewhere, the ground-floor had to contain the day-stairs by which the monks could reach their dormitory during daylight; the warming-house, with its one or more fire-places; and a passage to the infirmary quarters. In Cistercian monasteries the warming-house was situated near the refectory, as at **Fountains and Tintern.**

The Frater Range

The frater range flanked the alleyway directly opposite the church, except in Cistercian monasteries where, instead of running parallel to the cloister alley it was at right-angles to it. The frater, or refectory, was the monks' dining-hall, and internally it was similar to any medieval great hall. The entrance to it from the cloister was at its western end. Near this doorway, and along the cloister wall was the lavatorium (lavatory), where the monks washed their hands before going in to eat. This lavatory was usually a long stone trough set back into the frater wall of the cloister, as at **Rievaulx** and **Fountains.** At **Haughmond** and **Kirkham** it was in the west wall, and at **Gloucester** it was in the low inner cloister wall below the windows. **Much Wenlock, Exeter,** and **Canterbury** are some of the few English examples which followed the continental system of having a separate little pavilion centrally placed in the cloister garth, its basin fed by a pipe.

The monastic refectories of **Chester, Cleeve** and **Worcester** survive, while that of **Beaulieu** is now used as the parish church. In the refectory hall the tables would be parallel to the side walls, with the high table at the east end, where the chief monastic officers ate. There may have been a reredos behind this high table, and on a side wall close to it a pulpit from which one of the monks read aloud during meals. This reader's pulpit was reached by a stairway in the wall thickness, examples of this occurring at **Chester, Fountains** and **Shrewsbury.**

The eating of meat in the refectory was forbidden (but not bird-flesh), but as this observance, like so many others, was relaxed, particularly for sick brethren, special permission to eat meat was granted, but it had to be done in another room. So at some monasteries, second dining-halls were built, smaller than the main one, and called 'misericords'.

In Benedictine monasteries kitchens were built near the refectories, but standing free from them on the side away from the cloister. As at **Easby** and **Castle Acre** the kitchen was normally rectangular; at **Durham** it was polygonal. The fine and complete abbot's kitchen survives at **Glastonbury**, a square building with fireplaces diagonally in the angles, with arches carrying an octagonal vaulted roof.

Cistercian kitchens were near the cloister, placed so that meals prepared there could be served to the monks in the refectory and to the lay-brothers in their building. At **Fountains** the fireplaces were placed back-to-back in the centre of the kitchen, a door into the cloister near at hand simplifying the task of getting provision from the great cellar.

The cellarium, or cellar, was the great storehouse of the monastery, and formed the western range of the claustral buildings. As the outer court, or curia, through which provisions would enter the monastery, lay to the west, there is an obvious and practical reason for having the cellar in this western range, that of giving direct access. The cellar was usually the basement or undercroft of this western range, stone-vaulted from a row of central columns. At **Fountains**, the superb cellar has twenty-two bays and is double-aisled, part used as a cellar and a smaller part as a parlour between cloister and outer court.

In some of the Cistercian abbeys the upper floor of this western range formed a dormitory for the lay-brothers—as at **Fountains**—and in a number of monasteries of both Cistercian and Benedictine Orders it was divided into a number of rooms, for the head of the convent and for guests. together with, possibly, a chapel and also a common hall for servants of the monastery. Sometimes, where unorthodox arrangements had been forced upon the monastery through awkward lie of the land, as at **Durham** and **Easby,** the monks' dorter occupied this upper floor of the cellar range.

The Abbot's and the Guest's Lodgings

An abbot's quarters were similar to those of any other medieval lord, either ecclesiastical or lay. It must be remembered that the abbot of a great monastery was as important a patron of architecture as a great nobleman or a bishop, so the development of the design of his quarters, and those of his guests, was comparable to that of the big halls of medieval castles.

When the abbot's rooms were above the cellar range, they consisted of a hall, a chapel, and two or three other chambers. When, as occurred more often, they were not in this position, there was really no allotted site for them. At **Castle Acre** and **Chester** they were in a wing abutting on to the range nearest the church. At **Easby** the abbot's lodging was north of the church, and at **Haughmond** it was south of the cloisters; the priors of **Tynemouth** and **Lindisfarne** had quarters near the south end of the dorter range, as, later, did the prior of **Bolton.** At **Norwich** the guests were above the cellar range, and the bishop developed his own palace north of the church. Cistercian abbots tended to have lodgings south of the cloister, usually as a detached building, as at **Rievaulx** and **Fountains** (which, oddly, had prisoners' cells beneath it). One of the most characteristic examples of abbot's lodgings is at **Roche,** complete with its hall, kitchen, buttery, pantry, and other chambers.

Fountains retained two early examples of guest-houses as separate buildings a short way from the monastery, each of them having two floors, with each floor unequally divided into hall and chamber. **Bardney** and **Kirkstall** have aisled halls with chambers in cross-wings, and **Kirkstall** later grew to have its guest-houses as a complete self-contained unit round a small courtyard, with kitchen and stables.

The Infirmary Range

Sick monks, and those whose advancing years made them unable to cope with the severity of claustral life, were housed in the infirmary, which usually stood east of the cloister, thus being well away from any noise from the outer court to the west. Basically, it consisted of hall, chapel, and a kitchen providing a more appropriate diet than the normal monastic one. Some infirmaries had a special little frater of their own in which it was permitted to eat meat. The infirmarian also had two or three rooms as his own quarters.

The infirmaries of Benedictine monasteries were arranged rather like a church in plan, the hall being equivalent to the 'nave'. the inmates' beds occupying the 'aisles', and the infirmary chapel where the chancel would be, preferably correctly orientated west-east, like those of **Peterborough** and **Ely** and **Canterbury.**

Cistercian infirmaries developed to become a set of buildings grouped round its own little cloister, as at **Rievaulx** and **Tintern. Fountains** had a huge infirmary hall, 180 feet long by 80 feet wide, some of the columns of which still stand. Its chapel, kitchen, and infirmarer's house lay to the east. In sharp contrast is the fact that Premonstratensian infirmaries did not have chapels at all. Some Cistercian ones—**Roche** and **Jervaulx** among them—had a second infirmary for the lay-brethren.

The Outer Court

The buildings of the outer court—that is, those not associated or connected with the church or the claustral buildings— were essentially those concerned with the running of a self-contained community. Their number and size depended on the size of the monastery, which could vary from, say, twenty inmates of a small priory to perhaps six or seven hundred in a big Cistercian abbey such as **Rievaulx.**

Most of the outer court buildings were probably timber-framed, so very few have survived. Foundation plans help to give us a picture—at **Fountains,** for example, brewhouses and bakehouses can be identified, and the mill is still working. In addition to these which were common to all monasteries, there would be an almonry (where charity was dispensed), a granary—and barns for storing the different types of grain, workshops (a big monastery like **Durham** or **Norwich** would have a permanent mason's shop, carpenter's workshop, and probably a draughtsman's room), a smithy, a slaughter-house, a hen-house, separate buildings for oxen, cows, calves, and pigs, and a dovecote for the monastic pigeons, although these were more likely to have been built on higher ground outside the monastic precincts, as at **Bruton,** in Somerset, the ruins of whose dovecote stand very conspicuously to the south of the town.

Monastic precincts were entered through the main gate-house, a building almost invariably at least two storeys high. The ground floor was taken up by the passage through the gatehouse, with archways front and back, broad ones for wheeled traffic, and smaller side-arches for foot-traffic. **Easby** and **Worksop** have these two arches, of different sizes, in cross-walls in the middle of the gate-passage. The porter who controlled movements through the gatehouse had access by a small doorway in one of the side-walls.

Many gatehouses still stand—indeed, at **Kingswood** (Glos.) and **Montacute** (Som.) they are the only monastic remains. Size varies greatly—**Kingswood's** is small and gabled, contrasting with the massive and handsome gatehouses at **Thornton, Battle, St. Albans,** and **Bury St. Edmunds.** The upper floors at **Ely** and **St. Albans** contained prisons, those at **York** and **Whalley** were chapels. Monasteries with very extensive precincts had more than one gatehouse—**Bury St. Edmunds** having four, two of which still stand, as do the two at St. Augustine's at **Canterbury. Furness Abbey** also had two on the precinct wall, one outside, and a fourth inside leading to the monks' cemetery. **Tintern** and **York** had additional gatehouses leading to their nearby rivers—and these were naturally called watergates.

A number of Benedictine monasteries had parish churches on, or very near, the line of the precinct wall. Where this occurred, the gatehouse was built close to the church, as at **Reading** and **Abingdon,** and in each of these instances there was also a lay infirmary, dedicated to John the Baptist, and under abbey administration, next door. Cistercian abbeys, having naves for lay bretheren and thus not serving parish purposes, frequently provided a special lay chapel outside the precinct wall. A number of these have survived through becoming parish churches after the Dissolution, as at **Rievaulx.**

Outside the Precinct

Many monastic buildings lay beyond its walls, and these were usually concerned with its provisioning, and the running of its estates. Huge amounts of fish were needed for the monks, so, wherever they could, monasteries acquired fishing rights in both sea-waters and fresh waters. **St. Dogmael's** had the rights on the river Teifi, **Chester** had a boat on the river Dee, plus another, with ten nets, off Anglesey. In the low-lying lands of mid-Somerset at Meare, **Glastonbury Abbey** built the fourteenth century fish-house as the home and work-place-cum-store of the abbot's fisherman, whose job it was to look after the abbey fisheries which were centred on the 300-acre Meare Pool. Nearby is the Manor Farm, built at the same time as the fish-house, as a summer home for the abbot of **Glastonbury,** while in Cheshire is Saighton Grange, fulfilling the same purpose for the abbots of **Chester.**

Granges were monastic farms. The biggest ones, like that of **Minster-in-Thanet,** were almost miniature monasteries. The well-known village of **Grange-in-Borrowdale** in the Lake District arises from its once having been the site of the 'grange farm' of the monks of **Furness Abbey**, who farmed much of that valley from 1211 to the Dissolution.

Monasteries were great landowners, either of lands close to the abbeys themselves, as at **Glastonbury, Abbotsbury,** and **Whitby,** or of more outlying possessions. For example, the abbess of **Shaftesbury,** in Dorset, held a lot of land in Wiltshire, the produce of which was stored in the great medieval tithe barns at **Tisbury** and **Bradford-on-Avon.**

Monasteries, especially those with shrines, attracted many medieval pilgrims. Roadside chapels were built for them, the most outstanding being the Slipper Chapel near **Walsingham.** A lesser-known, and quite humble one is at **Chapel Plaister,** north of Bradford-on-Avon, for pilgrims Glastonbury-bound. At **Glastonbury** is the famous George and Pilgrims Inn, where they could stay, while **Gloucester** and **Canterbury** also have fine inns for medieval pilgrims to the abbeys. One unusual survival, also at **Glastonbury,** is the Abbot's Tribunal, the building where the abbot held his court and dealt with matters of law-keeping and law-breaking connected with his vast estates.

Charterhouses

Carthusian priories, by the very nature of the rigidly austere Rule of their Order, differed in many ways from those of the other Orders already described. Of the nine Carthusian priories founded in England one in particular, **Mount Grace,** in North Yorkshire, offers the best opportunity to study the lay-out, almost in its entirety.

The Carthusian plan necessitated there being at least two courtyards in the arrangements. The outer one, entered through a gatehouse, contained the usual buildings associated with an outer court—stables, barns and a guest-house, which, at **Mount Grace,** became a private house in 1654. This outer court led to very tiny court, with the cells of the prior and the sacrist, the chapter-house on the east of this tiny cloister, with, next to it, the aisleless presbytery of the small, plain church. This range of buildings, together with the frater for use only on occasional days, separated the outer court from the large cloister garth to the north, of which it formed one side—the south one.

This great cloister, at **Mount Grace,** is not square. Its northwest side is 272 feet, the other three are 231 feet each; no sides are parallel and no angles equal! The separate cells of the monks were small, two-storeyed cottages placed at intervals round this great cloister. Each cell was 27 feet square, with a doorway leading on to the cloister. Inside, the ground floor was divided to give a living-room, bedroom, study, and small oratory, while the upper floor was used as a workshop. Most of his meals being eaten alone, the monk received his food through an L-shaped hatch in the cottage wall facing the cloister garth. It was this shape so that neither the server from the kitchen nor the monk inside could see each other. A piped water supply led to each cell, and each one stood inside its own walled garden, at the far end of which was a tiny privy, outlet from which was to a continuous drain running round the outside of the claustral buildings.

The arrangement of the single cells, one of which has been reconstructed at **Mount Grace,** allowed the Carthusian monks not only to dwell apart from the world, but also to live a hermit-like existence apart from one another. Refectory meals were eaten only on Sunday and festivals, and the Carthusian monk would attend church only once or twice each day. The rest of his time he would spend alone in his cell, or working in his little garden.

In the **London** charterhouse there are some remains of cell doorways and service hatches. **Hinton Charterhouse** is the name of the village and the charterhouse a few miles south of Bath, where the finest remains are those of the chapter-house, perfectly preserved. The site of the two cloisters has been shown by excavation.

Friaries

The houses of friars differed again from those of the other Orders, primarily because they were more like missionary headquarters than permanent homes. They were very largely in towns, where they arrived a long time after the towns had themselves taken shape. Thus, the friaries were situated on any spare plot of land, in poor-quality buildings, sometimes little more than wooden huts, and often without a chapel. As both the Dominican and Franciscan friars became more numerous their Orders tended to adopt the more usual form of monastic lay-out, albeit distinctly simplified—church (large nave for preaching, small choir), small cloister, chapter-house, dorter and frater. The cloister was not used for study, and therefore was reduced to a single corridor; choir and nave were separated by a narrow passage beneath a slender tower; and the main entrance lay to the north of the church. Most friaries vanished at the Dissolution, only the larger churches—**Norwich, Chichester,** and the **City of London**—remained.

THE DAILY LIFE

A monk's day was divided up, not by meal-times like our day is, but by the services of the church. There were eight of these, and, with variations from summer to winter, and from one Order to another, the basic framework of the monk's day was built round these services. It started and finished much earlier than ours—a monk would rise about 2 a.m. and go to bed about 6.30 p.m. in the winter, and 8 p.m. in summer.

Three of the eight church services occurred before daybreak—Matins shortly after rising, followed by Lauds and Prime, the monks remaining in the church throughout this time, although in some Orders monks were allowed back in their dormitories between Lauds and Prime. Three of the services were held during the day, at intervals of three hours, the services being called Tierce, Sext and None (three, six and nine). The other two services, Vespers and Compline, were held at sunset and just before bedtime.

After Prime, say between 7 a.m. and 8 a.m., was the time when monks read or meditated in the cloisters, before going up the day-stairs to their dormitory to exchange their night-shoes for their day-shoes, returning to the cloister to wash, and then going into church again. Some monks would be excused service so that they could carry on with some of the essential monastery business, such as helping in the refectory, or preparing to read there during the main meal of the day.

Tierce was the first daily service, and this was followed by Mass, during which lay-people were allowed in to the nave of the church. After Mass came the daily Chapter, held in the chapter-house, and attended only by the monks from that particular religious house, presided over by the abbot, or, if he was away, by the prior.

Chapter, then, was a private meeting, held behind locked doors, at which the temporal business of the monastery would be discussed. Psalms, collects, and the day's martyrology were read, followed by the abbot's sermon. Any monkish misdemeanours would then be reported to the abbot or prior, confessions heard, and punishments, where merited, would be meted out. Some of these were very harsh, and Benedictine and Cistercian Rule allowed for corporal punishment to be administered, a birch-rod being used.

Chapter would last until about 10 a.m., and was followed by a period of work until noon, when the monks returned to church for Sext, with High Mass immediately afterwards. None would be held between 2 p.m. and 3 p.m., after which came the first—and main—meal of the day, held in the refectory, or frater. This would be presided over by the abbot, prior, or senior monk, seated at high table on a raised dais at the upper end of the room. During the meal the day's reader would go into the pulpit at the side of the room and read from a chosen work.

In Cistercian houses this main meal—dinner—consisted of a pound of bread and two courses of vegetables, probably cooked without fat. In Benedictine monasteries, and in Cistercian ones later on, when Rules became more relaxed, all sorts of fish, pastry, vegetables, cheese, wines, and milk were set before the monks. Special festivals would see the addition of pork pies and capons, blancmange and fruit tarts, and, as time went on, menus started to include poultry, salmon, eels, sides of beef or mutton, venison, oysters, spiced vegetables, butter, and eggs.

After dinner most monks studied or worked. In houses other than Cistercian, servants and peasant labour carried out the manual tasks in the monastery, as well as working in the garden or on the farm lands, thus leaving the monks themselves to concentrate on reading or writing, carving or painting, or tending the sick in the monastery's infirmary. Young monks and novices were even allowed the recreation offered by a game of bowls or skittles.

Vespers would be sung in church about 6 p.m., or earlier in winter, followed by a very light supper of bread and fruit, with a drink of ale. Night-shoes, which were warmer than day-shoes, would by now have been put on, and the monks would be summoned by the church bell to the last service of the day, Compline, after which they would return to their dorter in procession, and retire to bed until roused again by the bell for Matins, when they would descend by the night-stairs to the church for the daily round of church services again.

On fast days and throughout Lent the Rule of all Orders permitted only one meal a day, and that in the evening. It has to be remembered that the monastic Rules were worked out either in Italy or in France for the conditions which obtained there, and they were not altered to allow for the harsher conditions of the more northern latitudes in England. A monk's life was a hard and very strict one, and it is quite remarkable that the whole story of our monasteries is not largely one of attempts to evade the Rule, and the punishments which ensued. The monastic discipline not only survived throughout four and a half centuries, but succeeded in producing men of great wisdom and learning, having both intellectual and spiritual power, men whose leadership and guidance helped to shape our history.

It has also to be remembered that, throughout the Middle Ages, monasteries were not only centres of religious and civilized life, but served the community around them as church, hospital, school, library, farm, business centre, and inn. Spiritual fortresses in a savage world they were most certainly, they were not all, and not always, the islands of quiet sanctity their present appearances might suggest. The bigger monasteries in particular must have been full of interesting activity.

MONASTERIES AND THE LANDSCAPE

The extent to which monasteries in the Middle Ages helped to change the landscape is not often realised. The twelfth and thirteenth centuries saw much reclamation of marsh and fen land, in Lincolnshire, Somerset, and Kent, by the monasteries of Peterborough, Ely and Crowland, Glastonbury, Muchelney and Athelney, and by Canterbury Cathedral Priory. The reclaimed marshes then carried thousands of sheep—but even these flocks were only a fraction of those run by the Cistercian monasteries on northern hills and moors, and the wolds and downlands of the southern counties. The French abbey of Caen had 1500 sheep grazing Minchinhampton Common in the Cotswolds; **Fountains** owned at least 15,000 sheep on the Pennines, **Rievaulx** almost as many on the Yorkshire Moors, **Tintern** over 2,000 on Welsh hills, and **Neath** over 4,000, all in the thirteenth century. Sheep-farming on this scale followed almost ranch-like lines, and was operated from the many granges which were built by the Cistercians on their outlying estates, Boundary walls were built to separate the monastic estates, and these medieval walls formed the basis of the later walls, many of which still delineate the upland landscapes of the Yorkshire Dales and of Wales. Cistercians also cleared many woodlands in fertile vales, such as the Vale of York, where arable granges were established.

In some parts of the country the monastic buildings themselves would be a common and a grand sight. By 1350, the hey-day of monastic building, there were probably at least 800 monasteries of various Orders and sizes. In Yorkshire alone there were 66, and in Lincolnshire 51, with over 40 each in Kent, Somerset, and Gloucester. The number of monks, nuns, and canons at this time probably exceeded 15,000, but this quickly started to fall after the middle of the fourteenth century, for it was from then that the Cistercian lay-brothers vanished from the scene.

THE DISSOLUTION

There was a slow decline in the number of monasteries from the middle of the fourteenth century onwards. Anglo-French wars had contributed to this in that they created obvious difficulties of communication between the parent abbeys in France (Citeaux, Cluny and Premontre) with their daughter foundations in England of the Cistercian, Cluniac and Premonstratensian Orders. The Cluniacs suffered most in this respect, and a number had forcibly become independent priories.

By the fifteenth century many small houses had simply become too inadequate to exist—especially some of the Augustinian Canons, and they just faded out. **Longleat** in Wiltshire was one example, and its lands were handed over to the Carthusians at **Hinton.** Some small and inefficient priories were deliberately run down by bishops who were more concerned with reforms and learning, for which new buildings were needed. Jesus College, Cambridge, was once a nunnery, while St. John's College, Cambridge was augmented by the suppression of two small nunneries. Cardinal Wolsey's plans to found colleges at Oxford and Ipswich resulted in the suppression of twenty nine houses of monks, canons, or nuns, between 1524 and 1529. Among these were **Bayham, Daventry** and **St. Frideswide** at Oxford, whose site became that of Cardinal College, and whose church is now the College Chapel, and Cathedral of Christ Church, Oxford.

But by 1530 hundreds of monasteries still existed successfully, still well populated, and with their services devoutly carried out. Many buildings had been rebuilt, or were due for rebuilding, but a lot of monasteries had by now fallen considerably below their former high ideals, and the conduct of many monastic officials could justly be criticised, and in a few cases was quite infamous.

A report on the state and conditions and finances of the monasteries was made by Royal Commissioners for Henry VIII and his chief minister Thomas Cromwell. There is no doubt that the Commissioners often took care to discover what the king wanted them to about monastic faults and weaknesses. Reforms may have been necessary to the monastic system, but instead of this there was virtual revolution. The *Valor Ecclesiasticus* gave the king the fullest details of the endowed values of monastic lands and properties, together with their revenues. He acted on it, and the first basis for the suppression of the monasteries was an Act of Parliament of 1536 by which the smaller religious houses—those with a net annual income of under £200 were to be dissolved, the property and income going to the Crown, and the inmates transferred to larger houses, or pensioned off.

It was in the north of England that monasteries so dissolved were most missed. Poor people who had benefited from their charities suffered, especially after bad harvests, and they wanted the monasteries back. They set out for London on the Pilgrimage of Grace, hoping to see the king and ask for the removal of his hated adviser, Cromwell. Some monasteries, with their abbots, became involved, but the rising was met by the king's representative long before it reached London. He promised the rebels a free pardon, invited their leader to London, but by then it seemed likely to the rebels that nothing would come of their efforts, so they went home. Many were subsequently executed.

This threat prompted the king to further action against the remaining monasteries, and the Suppression Act of 1539 saw the Dissolution of the Monasteries into its final stages, the last ones being the biggest foundations, and continuing until 1540 with the surrender of **Waltham Abbey.** By then, some 5,000 monks, 2,000 canons regular, and 2,000 nuns had been pensioned off. Others had been appointed to various benefices, a few who had openly resisted the Suppression Acts were executed, and the monastic buildings and estates passed into the king's hands, later to be sold to rich laymen.

Some monastic churches became the basis for new bishop-rics—at **Bristol, Chester, Gloucester, Oxford, Peterborough** and temporarily, **Westminster**—where they achieved cathedral status. The cathedral priories became secular collegiate cathedrals, except for **Bath** and **Coventry.** The county lists at the end of this book indicate the numbers of collegiate cathedrals formed from the former cathedral priories.

Numerically more important was the total, or partial, preservation of many monastic churches. In a number of these the nave had already been used as a parish church, and the Dissolution did allow for parishioners to retain the nave for their own continued use, while the choir and transepts would be left to decay and collapse, or were deliberately destroyed. At **Malmesbury, Chepstow, Binham, Waltham, Leominster, Wymondham, Blyth, Shrewsbury, Thorney, Lanercost, Dunstable** and **Worksop** the nave is in use as the parish church; at **Crowland** it is the north aisle; at **Pershore** the parishioners exchanged the nave for the much finer chancel; at **Cartmel** only the south chancel aisle was used as the parish church, and is still known as the Town Choir. At **Bolton Priory** the nave is now the parish church, the chancel is in ruins. **Christchurch Priory** and **Selby Abbey** have survived in their entirety more by accident than intention of parishioners; by contrast, **Tewkesbury Abbey** survives complete as a church because the parishioners were not satisfied with only the nave, and they raised the £453 needed to buy the whole structure. **Dorchester Abbey** church is complete because one man, Richard Bewfforest, was generous enough to buy it—for £140 —and bequeath it to the parishioners.

Many monasteries eventually passed into the hands of laymen, and were wholly or partly demolished for the building materials they offered. Some were converted into fine country houses or large farms—**Cleeve, Lacock, Muchelney, Forde, Coverham, Much Wenlock, Woodspring, Milton Abbas, Stoneleigh.** It is usually the claustral buildings that were turned into houses, but at **Woodspring** the monastery church became the basis for the farmhouse.

BIBLIOGRAPHY

The Department of the Environment's official guidebooks to the various religious houses in their care are recommended for their authoritative and clear accounts, together with excellent layout plans. Their general guide is:

Abbeys: An Introduction to the Religious Houses of England and Wales. HMSO.

Other useful books are:

Butler, L. and Given-Wilson, c. *Medieval Monasteries of Great Britain.* Michael Joseph, 1978.

Cook, G. H. *English Monasteries in the Middle Ages.* 1961.

Crossley, F. H. *The English Abbey.* Batsford (revised 1962 by Bryan Little).

Dickinson, J. C. *Monastic Life in Medieval England.* Black, 1961.

Knowles, D. *The Monastic Order in England.* 1940.

Knowles, D. *The Religious Orders in England* (3 volumes). 1948, 1955 and 1959. (The most authoritative and comprehensive treatment of the whole subject.)

Knowles, D. and St Joseph, J. K. *Monastic Sites from the Air.* Cambridge, 1952.

Vale, Edmund. *Abbeys.* Batsford: Junior Heritage Book.

The Ordnance Survey Map of Monastic Britain (two sheets) is extremely valuable.

Monasticism in this country did not end with the Dissolution. Indeed, there are more than a dozen monasteries existing to-day, most of them of the Benedictine Order. As in the days of the medieval monasteries today's monks take their vows and give their lives to God, sometimes in seclusion from the world, and in others through work as well as prayer. Some twentieth century monasteries are kept going by the sale of goods made, and most of them welcome visitors and pilgrims who are genuinely interested in their work.

Ampleforth, near York, is a Benedictine community, together with a fine school, descended from the foundation at Westminster.

Aylesford Priory, near Maidstone, Kent. The present Carmelite Priory of friars occupies the site of the first Carmelite Priory in England. Fine pottery is made.

Belmont, Herefordshire, has an early Victorian church for its Benedictines.

Buckfast Abbey, Devon, a Benedictine monastery occupying since 1882 the site of the medieval monastery. The new church of the abbey was finished in 1938 after 31 years of work, built by the monks themselves.

Caldey Island, off the Pembrokeshire coast reached by boat from Tenby. The Cistercian monks grow their own produce, and sell some, and the medieval priory buildings are still used.

Douai, near Reading, is Benedictine.

Downside Abbey, near Bath, Avon, has the biggest and stateliest monastic church of this century, started in late Victorian times. Buildings of the famous school adjoin. Benedictine.

Farnborough, Hants, a Benedictine monastery, where monks design Christmas Cards and rear silkworms.

Mount St Bernard, near Loughborough, Leicestershire, is a Cistercian foundation in Charnwood Forest, where monks have their own farm and make pottery.

Prinknash, in the Cotswolds near Gloucester, established in 1928 by Benedictine monks in a Tudor manor house. Fine new monastic buildings were opened in 1972. The monastery is largely self-supporting from the estate produce and the sale of its famous pottery.

Quarr, on the Isle of Wight, is Benedictine, with a church designed by a monk.

Ramsgate, Kent, has a Benedictine monastery.

GAZETTEER OF THE MORE IMPORTANT MONASTIC REMAINS

* Indicates that all or part of the building is in the care of the Department of the Environment and is accessible to the public at normal times, on payment of a fee.

Many of the religious houses in this list that are *not* under the care of the Department of the Environment can be seen without difficulty by the public. But inclusion in this list does not guarantee that this is always the case.

The list includes many parish churches which were originally monastic churches or some other part of monastic buildings.

Other abbreviations:

A	Augustinian Canons (Black Canons)
B	Benedictines
Bons	Bonshommes
C	Cistercians
Car	Carthusians
Cl	Cluniacs
F	Friary
G	Gilbertines
N	Nunnery (e.g. BN Benedictine nuns)
P	Premonstratensians (White Canons)

ENGLAND

AVON

B	Bath Abbey (formerly Cathedral Priory)	Church in use.
A	Bristol Cathedral (formerly Abbey)	Part of the church, chapter house, and some domestic remains.
B	Bristol, St James's Priory	Nave in use.
F	Bristol, Dominican Priory	Important domestic remains.
Car	Hinton Charterhouse Priory	Chapter house.
A	Woodspring Priory (National Trust)	Part of church now a house (Landmark Trust).

BEDFORDSHIRE

A	Dunstable Priory	Nave in use.
BN	Elstow Abbey	Nave in use.

BERKSHIRE

B	Hurley Priory	Church in use.
B	Reading Abbey	Ruins.

BUCKINGHAMSHIRE

A	Chetwode Priory	Part of church in use.
C	Medmenham Abbey	Ruins.

CAMBRIDGESHIRE

A	Cambridge, Barnwell Priory	Gate chapel and domestic remains.
B	Cambridge, Buckingham College	Court surviving in Magdalene College.
BN	Cambridge, St Radegund's Priory	Church and some buildings in Jesus College.
F	Cambridge, Dominican Priory	Remains in Emmanuel College.
Fr N *	Denny Abbey	Important remains.
B	Ely Cathedral	Church and domestic remains.
B	* Isleham Priory	Ruins.
B	Peterborough Cathedral (formerly Abbey)	Church.
B	Thorney Abbey	Nave in use.

CHESHIRE

B	Chester Cathedral (formerly Abbey)	Church and extensive domestic remains.
A	Norton Priory	Some remains.

CLEVELAND

A	* Guisborough Priory	Ruins.

CORNWALL

A	St German's Priory	Nave in use.

CUMBRIA

C	Calder Abbey	Extensive ruins.
A	Carlisle Cathedral	Church, frater, undercroft.
A	Cartmel Priory	Church in use; gateway (National Trust).
C	* Furness Abbey	Very extensive remains.
C	Holm Cultram Abbey	Part of nave in use.
A	* Lanercost Priory	Nave in use, other buildings ruined.
P	* Shap Abbey	Ruins, fine setting, good tower.

DEVON

C	Buckland Abbey	Church became mansion, now part of Plymouth City Museum.

BN	Exeter, Polslo Priory	Domestic remains.
B	Exeter, St Nicholas's Priory	Some buildings survive.
A	Frithelstock Priory	Ruins.
B	Tavistock Abbey	Considerable remains.
P	Torquay, Torre Abbey	Important remains.

DORSET
B *	Abbotsbury Abbey	Ruins, chapel, tithe barn.
C	Bindon Abbey	Ruins, now part of country house.
B	Cerne Abbas	Gatehouse and tithe barn.
A	Christchurch Priory	Church in use.
C	Forde Abbey	Now a country mansion, with important remains inside.
B	Milton Abbey	Choir, transepts in use.
B	Sherborne Abbey	Church in use. Other buildings now part of school. Water conduit in town.

DURHAM
B	Durham Cathedral	Church, and very important domestic remains.
P *	Egglestone Abbey	Ruins.
B *	Finchale Priory	Ruins.

EAST SUSSEX
B *	Battle Abbey	Claustral remains. Very fine gateway.
P *	Bayham Abbey	Extensive ruins.
Cl	Lewes Priory	Scanty remains.
A	Michelham Priory	Gatehouse and other remains.

ESSEX
B *	Colchester Abbey	Ruins, gateway.
A *	Colchester, St Botolph's Priory	Ruins of nave (Roman brickwork).
A	Little Dunmow Priory	Part of church in use.
A	St Osyth's Priory	Gatehouse, other buildings now a house.
Cl	Southend, Prittlewell Priory	Remains.
C	Tilty Priory	Lay chapel now parish church.
A	Waltham Abbey	Nave in use. Gatehouse.

GLOUCESTERSHIRE
| B | Deerhurst Priory | Nave in use. |
| C | Flaxley Abbey | Important domestic remains. |

B	Gloucester Cathedral (formerly Abbey)	Church. Very important domestic remains, with carrells in cloisters, and monks' lavatorium.
F	Gloucester, Dominican Priory	Part of church is now a house; important domestic remains.
F	Gloucester, Franciscan Priory	Part of church remains.
A	Gloucester, St Oswald's Priory	Church ruins.
C *	Hailes Abbey	Ruins.
C	Kingswood Abbey	Fine gatehouse.
B	Leonard Stanley Priory	Church in use.
B	Tewkesbury Abbey	Church in use.
B	Winchcombe Abbey	Some remains.

HAMPSHIRE

C	Beaulieu Abbey	Ruins, west range, frater now used as parish church.
C *	Netley Abbey	Extensive remains.
BN	Romsey Abbey	Church in use.
P *	Titchfield Abbey	Extensive remains; gatehouse.
B	Winchester Cathedral	Church only.

HEREFORD AND WORCESTER

C	Abbey Dore	Chancel, transepts in use.
B	Evesham Abbey	Ruins; good bell tower.
B	Great Malvern Priory	Church in use; gateway.
B	Leominster Priory	Nave in use.
B	Little Malvern Priory	Chancel in use.
B	Pershore Abbey	Chancel, south transept in use.
B	Worcester Cathedral	Church; good monastic remains.

HERTFORDSHIRE

A	Royston Priory	Church in use (partly).
B	St Albans Cathedral (formerly Abbey)	Church; very fine gateway.
BN	Sopwell (St Albans)	Ruins.

HUMBERSIDE

A	Bridlington Priory	Nave in use; gateway.
CN	Swine Priory	Chancel in use.
A *	Thornton Abbey	Ruins; very fine gateway.
G	Watton Priory	Site of this rare double house has been excavated; prior's house is in use.

KENT

F	Aylesford	Important remains; now occupied by Carmelites.
C	Boxley	Monastic barn.
B	Canterbury Cathedral	Church; monastic buildings.
B	∗ Canterbury, St Augustine's Abbey	Gateways; other remains.
F	Canterbury, Dominican Friary	Considerable remains.
B	Dover Priory	Guest house and frater now part of College.
BN	Malling Abbey	Important ruins. Benedictine nuns now occupy the site (Anglican).
BN	Minster (Sheppey)	Church in use.
B	Rochester Cathedral	Church; some domestic ruins.
P	St Radegund's Abbey	Extensive ruins.

LANCASHIRE

P	Cockersand Abbey	Ruins, except chapter-house.
B	Lancaster Priory	Church in use.
C	∗ Salley Abbey, Sawley	Extensive remains; gateway.
B	Upholland Priory	Choir used as church.
C	Whalley Abbey	Extensive ruins; gatehouses.

LEICESTERSHIRE

A	Ulverscroft Priory	Important ruins.

LINCOLNSHIRE

B	Bardney Abbey	Ruins.
A	Bourne Priory	Nave in use.
B	Crowland Abbey	North aisle in use; other good remains.
B	Deeping, St James's Priory	Nave in use.
B	Freiston Priory	Nave in use.
C	Kirkstead Abbey	Gate chapel in use.
G	Sempringham	Nave in use.

LONDON

BN	Bishopsgate, St Helen's	Church in use.
Car	Charterhouse	Important remains part of Sutton's Hospital; chapter-house.
A	Smithfield, St Bartholomew's Priory	
A	Southwark Cathedral (formerly the Priory of St Mary Overy)	Transepts, choir.

B	Westminster Abbey	Church, monastic buildings.

MERSEYSIDE

B	Birkenhead Priory	Ruins; chapter house now a chapel.

NORFOLK

B	* Binham Priory	Nave in use.
F	Burnham Norton	Ruins.
Cl	* Castle Acre Priory	Very important remains, gatehouse.
A	* Creake Abbey	Ruins.
B	Norwich Cathedral	Church, cloisters, some domestic remains.
F	Norwich, Dominican Friary	Church now in use as public hall.
Cl	* Thetford Priory	Considerable remains.
A	Walsingham Priory	Ruins.
B	Wymondham Abbey	Nave in use.

NORTHAMPTONSHIRE

A	Canons Ashby Priory	Nave in use.

NORTHUMBERLAND

P	Blanchland Abbey	Nave and transept in use; gateway.
A	Brinkburn Priory	Church complete.
A	Hexham Priory	Church in use; best example of night stairs in country.
B	* Lindisfarne Priory	Considerable ruins.
C	Newminster Abbey	Ruins.

NORTH YORKSHIRE

A	Bolton Priory	Nave in use; choir ruined; fine setting.
C	* Byland Abbey	Extensive ruins.
P	Coverham Abbey	Ruins, incorporated into house.
P	* Easby Abbey	Very extensive ruins.
C	Fountains Abbey	Finest, most extensive Cistercian ruins in country.
C	Jervaulx Abbey	Extensive ruins.
A	* Kirkham Priory	Ruins, gateway.
G	Malton Priory	Nave in use.
Car	* Mount Grace Priory	Most important Carthusian ruins in country.

BN	Nun Monkton	Nave in use.
C	* Rievaulx Abbey	Extensive and splendid ruins; setting.
B	Selby Abbey	Church in use.
B	* Whitby Abbey	Extensive ruins in fine setting.
B	York, St Mary's Abbey	Ruins, fortifications.
B	York, Holy Trinity Priory	Nave in use.

NOTTINGHAMSHIRE

B	Blyth Priory	Nave in use.
G	* Mattersey Priory	Ruins.
A	Newstead Priory	Now a country house.
C	Rufford Abbey	Claustral remains.
A	Thurgarton Priory	Nave in use.
A	Worksop Priory	Nave in use; fine gateway.

OXFORDSHIRE

B	Abingdon Abbey	Gatehouse, and domestic buildings.
A	Dorchester Abbey	Church in use.
A	Oxford Cathedral (formerly St Frideswide's Priory)	Church; some domestic buildings.
B	Oxford, Durham Hall	Some surviving buildings in Trinity College.
B	Oxford, Gloucester Hall	Some buildings surviving in Worcester College.
C	Oxford, St Bernard's College	Some buildings surviving in St John's College.

SHROPSHIRE

B	Bromfield Priory	Nave in use. Gatehouse.
C	* Buildwas Abbey	Considerable ruins.
A	* Haughmond Priory	Considerable ruins. Monk's well.
A	* Lilleshall Abbey	Extensive remains.
Cl	* Much Wenlock Priory	Excellent remains; prior's lodging.
B	Shrewsbury Abbey	Nave in use.
AN	* White Ladies Priory, Boscobel	Ruins.

SOMERSET

C	* Cleeve Abbey	Especially fine domestic remains.
B	Dunster Priory	Church in use.
B	Glastonbury Abbey	Considerable ruins; fine monks' kitchen.
B	* Muchelney Abbey	Domestic remains.

A	Stavordale Priory	Church survives as a farmhouse.
AP	Stogursey Priory	Church in use.
Car	Witham Priory	Gate chapel in parochial use.

SOUTH YORKSHIRE
B	*Monk Bretton Priory	Ruins.
C	*Roche Abbey	Considerable ruins.

STAFFORDSHIRE
C	*Croxden Abbey	Ruins.
B	Tutbury Priory	Nave in use.

SUFFOLK
B	*Bury St Edmunds Abbey	Ruins; fine gateways.
A	*Herringfleet, St Olave's Priory	Fine crypt.
P	Leiston Abbey	Considerable remains.

SURREY
A	Newark Priory	Ruins.
C	Waverley Abbey	Scanty ruins.

TYNE AND WEAR
B	*Jarrow Priory	Claustral remains. Church of Saxon monastery.
F	Newcastle, Dominican Friary	Considerable remains.
B	*Tynemouth Priory	Extensive ruins.

WARWICKSHIRE
A	Maxstoke Priory	Gateway and tower.
C	Merevale Abbey	Gate chapel in use.

WEST MIDLANDS
P	Halesowen Abbey	Ruins.

WEST SUSSEX
B	Boxgrove Priory	Chancel in use.
F	Chichester, Franciscan Friary	Choir remains.

WEST YORKSHIRE
C	Kirkstall	Splendid ruins.

WILTSHIRE
BN	Amesbury Priory	Church in use.

Bons	Edington Priory	Splendid priory church of this rare Order, which had only two English houses.
AN	Lacock Abbey (National Trust)	Fine remains, especially cloisters, all now incorporated into country mansion.
B	Malmesbury Abbey	Nave in use.

WALES

CLWYD
| C | * Basingwerk Abbey | Ruins. |
| C | * Valle Crucis Abbey | Extensive remains. |

DYFED
C	St Dogmael's Abbey	Ruins of church (Tironian monks).
C	* Strata Florida Abbey	Some remains.
P	* Talley Abbey	Ruins.

GWENT
B	Abergavenny Priory	Church in use.
B	Chepstow Priory	Nave in use.
A	* Llanthony Priory	Important ruins.
C	* Tintern Abbey	Extensive and important ruins in very fine setting.
BN	Usk Priory	Nave in use; gatehouse.

GWYNEDD
| C | * Cymmer Abbey | Ruins. |
| A | Penmon Priory | Part of church in use; dovecote. |

MID GLAMORGAN
| B | Ewenny Priory | Nave in use; rest of church survives. |

POWYS
| B | Brecon Cathedral (formerly Priory) | Church in use. |

WEST GLAMORGAN
| C | Margam Abbey | Nave in use, rest ruins. |
| C | * Neath Abbey | Ruins. |

SCOTLAND

BORDERS
P	* Dryburgh Abbey	Considerable remains.
A	* Jedburgh Abbey	Splendid ruins.
C	* Kelso Abbey	Fine ruins (Tironian monks).
C	* Melrose Abbey	Splendid ruins.

CENTRAL
A	* Cambuskenneth Abbey	Bell-tower, some ruins.
A	* Inchmahome Priory	Extensive remains.

DUMFRIES AND GALLOWAY
C	* Dundrennan Abbey	Considerable remains.
C	* Glenluce Abbey	Some remains.
C	* Sweetheart Abbey	Splendid ruins.
B	* Whithorn Priory	Ruins.

FIFE
C	* Culross Abbey	Church in use.
B	Dunfermline Abbey	Some remains.
A	* Inchcolm Abbey	Some remains incorporated into house.
B	* St Andrew's Priory	Ruins.

GRAMPIAN
C	* Deer Abbey	Extensive ruins.

HIGHLAND
B	* Beauly Priory	Ruins.

STRATHCLYDE
B	* Ardchattan Priory	Ruins; part now an inhabited house.
Cl	* Crossraguel Abbey	Extensive ruins; fine gatehouse.

TAYSIDE
Cl	* Arbroath Abbey	Considerable remains, gatehouse tower.
A	* Restenneth Priory	Ruins.

INDEX

Abbey Dore 35
Abbotsbury 45
Abingdon 7, 44
Alnwick 11
Ampleforth 53
Aylesford 53
Bardney 42
Barking 11
Bath 3, 7, 51
Battle 44
Bayham 11, 50
Beaulieu 40
Belmont 53
Binham 36, 51
Blyth 36, 51
Bolton 11, 35, 42, 51
Bourne 37
Bradford-on-Avon 6, 45
Bridlington 36, 37
Bristol 11, 40, 51
Bruton 43
Buckfast 53
Buildwas 36, 37, 38
Bury St Edmunds 7, 13, 38, 44
Byland 36
Caldey Island 53
Canterbury 5, 6, 7, 37, 38, 40, 43, 44, 45, 49
Carlisle 11, 35
Cartmel 11, 36, 51
Castle Acre 10, 36, 39, 41, 42
Cerne 7
Chepstow 51
Chester 37, 38, 40, 41, 42, 44, 51
Chichester 46
Christchurch 11, 35, 52
Cleeve 38, 39, 40, 52
Cockersand 40
Colchester 11
Coventry 51
Coverham 52
Crowland 7, 49, 51
Daventry 50
Dorchester 11, 52
Douai 53
Downside 53
Dryburgh 3, 38
Dunstable 36, 51
Durham 6, 35, 36, 37, 39, 41, 43
Easby 11, 35, 39, 41, 42, 43
Egglestone 11
Elstow 36
Ely 7, 43, 44, 49
Evesham 37
Exeter 40
Eynsham 7
Farnborough 53
Forde 52
Fountains 9, 15, 35, 36, 37, 38, 40, 41, 42, 43, 49
Furness 9, 36, 40, 44, 45
Glastonbury 6, 7, 35, 36, 41, 44, 45, 49
Gloucester 35, 36, 37, 38, 40, 45, 51
Grange-in-Borrowdale 9, 45
Great Malvern 37
Haughmond 40, 42
Hexham 36
Hinton 10, 12, 40, 46, 50

Iona 5
Jarrow 6
Jervaulx 43
Kingswood 44
Kirkham 35, 39, 40
Kirstall 35, 42
Lacock 3, 12, 52
Lanercost 11, 51
Leominster 36, 51
Lewes 10, 39
Lindisfarne 6, 35, 42
London 11, 35, 46
Longleat 50
Malmesbury 3, 13, 37, 51
Milton Abbas 52
Minster-in-Thanet 44
Montacute 44
Mount Grace 10, 45-6
Mount St Bernard 53
Muchelney 49, 52
Much Wenlock 10, 36, 40, 52
Neath 49
Newminster 33
Norwich 35, 36, 42, 43, 46
Nun Monkton 36
Oxford 50, 51
Pershore 52
Peterborough 7, 36, 43, 49, 51
Prinknash 53
Quarr 53
Ramsgate 53
Reading 44
Rievaulx 3, 9, 35, 36, 38, 39, 40, 42, 43, 44, 49
Roche 36, 42, 43
Rochester 38
Romsey 3, 11, 12, 36, 37
St Albans 5, 15, 36, 44
St Dogmael's 44
Selby 3, 36, 52
Shaftesbury 45
Shap 11
Sherborne 3
Shrewsbury 41, 51
Stoneleigh 52
Syon 13
Tewkesbury 35, 36, 52
Thetford 10, 36
Thorney 51
Thornton 35, 44
Tintern 3, 38, 39, 40, 43, 44, 49
Tisbury 45
Titchfield 11
Tynemouth 36, 42
Valle Crucis 35, 39
Walsingham 45
Waltham 51
Waverley 8
Westminster 3, 13, 36, 37, 39, 40, 51
Whalley 44
Whitby 35, 45
Winchcombe 7
Winchester 7, 35, 36, 37
Woodspring 52
Worcester 7, 39, 40
Worksop 37, 43, 51
Wymondham 51
York 7, 35, 44